Overview *A World of Fish*

Fish of every size and kind live all around the world.

Reading Vocabulary Words

skeleton
predator
native

High-Frequency Words

fish	*have*
are	*some*
found	*sea*
live	*eat*

Building Future Vocabulary

* These vocabulary words do not appear in this text. They are provided to develop related oral vocabulary that first appears in future texts.

Words:	*sleek*	*bunch*	*zigzag*
Levels:	Library	Library	Library

Comprehension Strategy
Making generalizations

Fluency Skill
Pausing at commas

Phonics Skill
Identifying and reading compound words (infant/fish, fresh/water, some/times, water/birds, clown/fish, angel/fish, blue/fin)

Reading-Writing Connection
Drawing a picture

Home Connection
Send home one of the Flying Colors Take-Home books for children to share with their families.

Differentiated Instruction
Before reading the text, query children to discover their level of understanding of the comprehension strategy — Making generalizations. As you work together, provide additional support to children who show a beginning mastery of the strategy.

Focus on ELL
- Have children make drawings of fish. Point out and discuss features of the fish and help children associate them with the correct English terms.

- If possible, share pictures of lakes, ponds, rivers, and seas. Ask children to share where the fish they drew live and swim.

Using This Teaching Version

1. Before Reading

2. During Reading

3. Revisiting the Text

4. Assessment

This Teaching Version will assist you in directing children through the process of reading.

1. **Begin with Before Reading** to familiarize children with the book's content. Select the skills and strategies that meet the needs of your children.

2. **Next, go to During Reading** to help children become familiar with the text, and then to read individually on their own.

3. **Then, go back to Revisiting the Text** and select those specific activities that meet children's needs.

4. **Finally, finish with Assessment** to confirm children are ready to move forward to the next text.

Building Background

• Write the word *skeleton* on the board. Read the word aloud. Ask children to share what they know about skeletons and which creatures have them. Correct any misconceptions.

• Introduce the book by reading the title, talking about the cover photograph, and sharing the overview.

Building Future Vocabulary
Use Interactive Modeling Card: Classifying New Words

• Introduce the word *bunch*. Use it in a sentence. Explain that knowing how a word is used in a sentence can help readers understand the word. Using the chart, guide children to explore the word's use, then mark the appropriate column.

• Repeat with the words *sleek* and *zigzag*.

Introduction to Reading Vocabulary

• On blank cards write: *skeleton*, *predator*, and *native*. Read them aloud. Tell children these words will appear in the text of *A World of Fish.*

• Use each word in a sentence for understanding.

Introduction to Comprehension Strategy

- Explain that we make generalizations by combining important details and then drawing conclusions about them that go beyond the text.

- Tell children they will be stopping during reading to identify important details and discuss generalizations that can be made about them.

- Ask children what important details they can learn about the book from its cover.

Introduction to Phonics

- List on the board: **sometimes, freshwater, clownfish,** and **waterbirds.** Read the words aloud. Ask if children notice what is similar about all of the words. Point out that all are compound words.

- Ask volunteers to draw lines between the two words that make up each compound word. Discuss how the two words are combined to create a new word.

- Ask children for more examples of compound words. Write these on the board and have children identify the two original words in each.

- Have children look for other compound words as they read *A World of Fish.*

Modeling Fluency

- Read aloud page 10, modeling pausing at commas.

- Talk about the use of commas. Point out that this punctuation mark tells a reader to pause briefly.

2 During Reading

Book Talk

Beginning on page T4, use the During Reading notes on the left-hand side to engage children in a book talk. On page 24, follow with Individual Reading.

Book Talk

- Explain to children that every part of a book, including the table of contents, photographs, and text, contains information for the reader.

- **Comprehension Strategy**
Point to the table of contents and explain that it gives important details about each of the chapters. Ask *What detail do most of the chapters seem to be about?* (a place where fish live) *Based on the chapter titles, what can we conclude about what we'll learn in this book?* (Fish live in many different places.)

- Ask *Does one of these chapters sound interesting to you? What details are you curious to discover?*

Turn to page 2 – Book Talk

A World of Fish

Heather Hammonds

A World of Fish

Heather Hammonds

Future Vocabulary

- Have children look at the cover photograph. Draw attention to the tentacles. Ask *Why would the fish want to swim in the middle of a bunch of tentacles?* (The fish might be protected by the tentacles; maybe there is food for the fish in the tentacles.)

Now revisit pages 2–3

During Reading

Book Talk

- Hold up the word card for *skeleton*. Have children locate the word on page 3 and practice saying the word. Ask *Do fish have skeletons?* (yes) *What are fish skeletons made of?* (cartilage or bones) *Do you have a skeleton too?* (yes) *What is it made of?* (bones)

- **Phonics Skill** Have children point to each fish photograph and read the name in the caption. Ask children to identify names that are compound words. *(squirrelfish, sweetlip)*

Turn to page 4 – Book Talk

Chapter 1

Fantastic Fish

Fish are amazing water animals. They are found all around the world from the coldest places to the warmest places.

Some types of fish live in rivers, lakes, and ponds. Many fish live in the sea.

salmon

Hawaiian squirrelfish

2

Fish Bodies

Some fish have skeletons made of bone. Other fish have skeletons made of **cartilage**.

a dotted sweetlip

Most fish have fins. Fish also have **gills** for breathing.

great white shark

3

Future Vocabulary

- Have children review all the photographs on these pages. Ask *Which of the photographs show a bunch of fish?* (the ones on page 2 of the salmon and the Hawaiian squirrelfish) *Which bunch is bigger?* (the squirrelfish)

- Ask children if they have ever heard the term "bunched up." Tell them that *bunch* means a group of something. Say Bunched up *refers to a group, but it also means crowded together. Which bunch of fish looks bunched up?* (the squirrelfish)

- Ask *Have you ever seen a bunch of kids doing something together? Have you ever been bunched up?* Have children share experiences.

Now revisit pages 4–5

During Reading

Book Talk

- **Comprehension Strategy** Ask *What important details do we learn about fish on these pages?* (There are thousands of different kinds; some are big, some are small, some are colorful, some are powerful; the biggest fish is more than 41 feet long; the smallest fish is less than 1 centimeter long.) *What are most of these facts about?* (the size of fish) *What conclusion can we make about the size of fish from these facts?* (Fish are all different sizes.)

- **Phonics Skill** Have children locate the compound words on this page. *(clownfish, infantfish)* Ask *How do you think the clownfish got its name?* (It has bright colors, as if it is dressed up like a clown.) *How do you think the infantfish got its name?* (It is the smallest fish in the world, so it is named for a baby.)

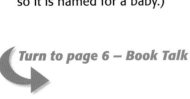

Turn to page 6 — Book Talk

an angelfish

There are thousands of different types of fish. Some fish are small and colorful, while others are large and powerful.

Porcupine fish can puff up like a ball!

4

a porcupine fish

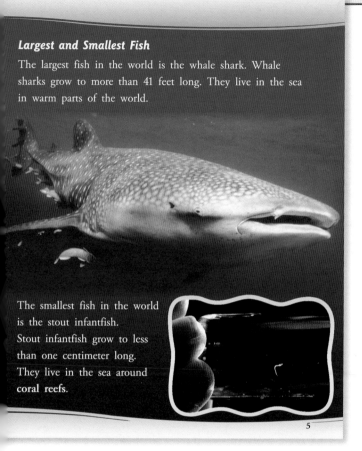

Largest and Smallest Fish

The largest fish in the world is the whale shark. Whale sharks grow to more than 41 feet long. They live in the sea in warm parts of the world.

The smallest fish in the world is the stout infantfish. Stout infantfish grow to less than one centimeter long. They live in the sea around **coral reefs.**

5

Future Vocabulary

- Ask *Are any of the fish on these pages in bunches?* (no) *Why not?* (None are in groups; each fish is alone.)

- Ask *Which fish look sleek and smooth?* (the clownfish, the shark) *Is the porcupine fish sleek?* (No, it has lots of points.) Encourage children to name other things that are sleek. Ask *What could you do to make your dog's fur look sleek?* (wash him, brush him)

Now revisit pages 6–7

During Reading

Book Talk

- **Phonics Skill** Read page 6 aloud, including captions, asking children to clap when they hear a compound word. Have children point to each of the compound words. *(freshwater, sockeye, goldfish)* Have them practice saying each word. Ask a volunteer to read the page aloud.

- Ask *Which of the fish pictured on this page have skeletons?* (all) *What other water animals have skeletons?* (whales, dolphins, seals)

Turn to page 8 – Book Talk

Chapter 2

Rivers, Lakes, and Ponds

Freshwater fish live in rivers, lakes, and ponds. They need clean, fresh water to survive.

Some large freshwater fish live in deep lakes and big rivers.

sockeye salmon

goldfish

Other smaller freshwater fish live in ponds in parks and gardens.

6

Northern Pike

Northern pike are very large, powerful freshwater fish that can grow to more than four feet long. They live in big, cold lakes and rivers in North America, Asia, and Europe.

Northern pike eat smaller fish and animals such as frogs. Sometimes they eat young waterbirds such as ducklings.

7

Future Vocabulary

• Say *The sockeye salmon are swimming above a* bunch *of rocks at the bottom of that river or lake. Some people keep a* bunch *of rocks in a collection. Do you have a* bunch *of anything in a collection? What?*

• Explain that *sleek* means smooth and shiny, but another meaning for the word is healthy-looking. Ask *Which fish on these pages do you think will soon be* sleek *and well-fed?* (the Northern pike, because it is eating)

Now revisit pages 8–9

During Reading

Book Talk

- **Fluency Skill** Read the first paragraph on page 8, modeling pausing at commas. Ask *How did I know when to pause?* (the commas) Point out that in the second sentence the author lists three different places where fish live. Explain that commas keep things in a list from running together. Ask a volunteer to read the sentence, pausing at commas. Have children practice reading the sentence with pauses.

- Hold up the word card for *native.* Have children locate the word on page 8 and practice saying it. Say *A person or animal is native to the place they are from. Do European carp live only in the place where they are native?* (No, they have spread to other places.) *Why are they pests in places where they are not native?* (They take the place of the native fish.)

Turn to page 10 – Book Talk

Some freshwater fish are found only in one part of the world. Murray cod live in the rivers, lakes, and streams in the eastern parts of Australia.

a Murray cod

European carp are found in many countries of the world. They have spread from the continent of Europe to other places. In some countries they are pests because they take the place of other **native** fish.

a European carp

8

Koi

Koi are a type of colorful fish from Japan. They are much bigger than goldfish and can live for more than 100 years.

Sometimes koi are called living jewels because they are so beautiful. People usually keep their koi in large garden ponds. The most beautiful koi cost thousands of dollars.

9

Future Vocabulary

- Ask *If you had a large garden pond at your house that you were going to fill with koi, would you want just one or two koi, or a bunch of koi? Why? Would you like to have a bunch of fish in a fish tank? Why or why not?*

Now revisit pages 10–11

During Reading

Book Talk

- **Fluency Skill** Have children locate the comma in the first sentence on page 10. Explain that authors sometimes use commas to separate ideas. Read the sentence aloud, modeling pausing at the comma. Ask children to identify the two ideas in the sentence. Have children read the sentence, pausing at the comma.

- Ask *Can freshwater fish be native to salty seas?* (no, because that's not where they are from) *Do all fish live only in the waters where they are native?* (No, some fish live in both freshwater and salty seas.)

Turn to page 12 – Book Talk

Chapter 3

From the Rivers to the Seas

Most freshwater fish live only in freshwater, and most **marine** fish live only in the sea. However some fish live in both freshwater rivers and salty seas at different times in their **life cycles**.

They swim from rivers to seas and from seas to rivers.

salmon

American eels

10

Salmon

Salmon hatch from eggs in rivers and streams.
As they grow, they swim down the rivers and streams and into the sea.

The salmon grow very big in the sea. When it is time for them to **breed,** they return to the river or stream where they were born. Female salmon lay eggs. The eggs hatch into more salmon.

11

Future Vocabulary

- Ask *When salmon swim from rivers to seas and from seas to rivers, do you think they swim straight or zigzag? Why? Do you ever zigzag when you're on the playground?*

Now revisit pages 12–13

During Reading

Book Talk

- **Comprehension Strategy**
Explain that words like *all, many, most, lots,* and *usually* often signal a generalization. Ask *Which word on this page signals a generalization? (lots) What generalization does the author make?* (Lots of fish live close to shore.) *How many details does the author give as examples that lots of fish live near the shore?* (two: small fish live in rock pools or hide in shallow water; some bigger fish live close to shore too)

Turn to page 14 – Book Talk

Chapter 4

By the Shore

Lots of fish live close to the shore or in places where rivers meet the sea.

Small fish can be found in rock pools or hiding in sea plants in **shallow** water.

Bigger fish sometimes live close to the shore, too.

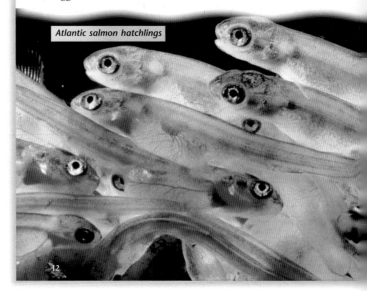

Atlantic salmon hatchlings

12

a baby elephant fish hatching from an egg case

Elephant Fish

Elephant fish live mostly in deep water in the sea. Each spring they swim closer to the shore. The female elephant fish lay special egg cases in the shallow water. Baby elephant fish hatch from the egg cases and grow. As they grow bigger, they move into deeper parts of the sea.

13

Future Vocabulary
- Remind children that *zigzag* means to move in a series of short, sharp turns or bends. Explain that *zigzag* can also be a noun or an adjective describing something with bends or sharp turns. Ask *Do you ever draw* zigzag *lines? Which of the fish shown has a* zigzag *nose?* (the elephant fish) *What makes it a* zigzag? (It has a sharp bend.)

Now revisit pages 14–15

During Reading

Book Talk

- Have children locate the word *predator* on page 15. Say *The great white shark is a fierce predator because it hunts for fish and large animals. What other animals are predators?* (lions, tigers, snakes)

- **Comprehension Strategy**
  Ask *What details do we learn about sharks on these pages?* (Their skeletons are cartilage; there are more than 450 kinds; some live close to shore, some deep at sea; most hunt fish and animals.) *Which of these details apply to most sharks?* (Their skeletons are made of cartilage; most sharks are hunters.) *Which of these details gives more information about what sharks are like?* (Most are hunters.) *Could we make a generalization about sharks by saying "sharks are predators"?* (yes)

Turn to page 16 – Book Talk

Sharks are a large group of marine fish that have skeletons made of cartilage.

There are more than 450 different kinds of sharks. Most sharks hunt fish and other sea animals.

Some sharks live close to the shore, and others live farther out at sea in deeper water.

grey reef sharks

14

Great White Shark

The great white shark is a fierce **predator**.

Sometimes great white sharks swim close to the shore when they are hunting for food.

They eat other fish as well as large sea animals, such as seals and sea lions.

15

Future Vocabulary

- Ask *Which photograph shows a bunch of sharks?* (the photograph on page 14) *Would you want to swim in the water with a bunch of sharks?* (no) *Why not?* (They're dangerous.)

Now revisit pages 16–17

During Reading

Book Talk

- **Phonics Skill** Have children find the compound word on page 16. *(underwater)* Have a volunteer read the chapter title aloud. Ask *What does the word* underwater *mean?* (under the water)

- Have children locate the word *predators* on page 17. Ask *Does the leafy sea dragon hide because it's a* predator *and it doesn't want the creatures it hunts to see it?* (No, it hides to stay safe from the *predators* that hunt it.)

Turn to page 18 – Book Talk

Chapter 5

Underwater Forests

In some places, not far from the shore, huge **kelp** forests grow beneath the waves.

The kelp grows very tall, just like trees on land. It is home to lots of different fish and other sea animals. The fish and other sea animals hide in the kelp.

16

16

Leafy Sea Dragon

Leafy sea dragons are small fish that live in some kelp forests.

Leafy sea dragons have special leafy frills on their bodies. The leafy frills make the fish very hard to see when they hide among the kelp. This helps keep them safe from predators.

17

Future Vocabulary

- Draw children's attention to the kelp in the photograph on page 17. Point out the berrylike air sacs growing on the plant. Ask *What words can we use to describe how these grow?* (in a bunch) *What other things grow in bunches?* (grapes, bananas)

- Ask *Could we describe the leafy sea dragon by saying it has a bunch of zigzag frills?* (yes) *Why?* (It has a lot of frills with sharp turns or bends.)

Now revisit pages 18–19

During Reading

Book Talk

- Ask *How could swimming in a school help fish stay safe from predators?* (It would be harder to attack fish in a big group.)

- **Phonics Skill** Draw attention to the word *bluefin.* Ask *Is bluefin a compound word?* (yes) *How can you tell?* (It's made up of two smaller words, *blue* and *fin.*) Have children read page 19 aloud to practice reading the compound word.

- **Fluency Skill** Have children find and point to the commas on page 18. Remind them not to rush past commas, but to take time to pause. Read the first sentence, modeling the pauses. Have children read the rest of the page aloud.

Turn to page 20 — Book Talk

Chapter 6

Out in the Sea

Lots of fish live out in the sea, far away from land. They swim quickly through the water, hunting for food, such as other smaller fish.

Some fish travel together in large groups called schools. Schools of fish often swim long distances across the sea.

Atlantic mackerel

18

Southern Bluefin Tuna

Southern bluefin tuna are large, powerful fish that swim long distances in the sea.

During the day the tuna hunt for food far beneath the waves. They eat small fish and other water creatures.

Sometimes southern bluefin tuna even eat other smaller tuna.

19

Future Vocabulary

- Ask *Is it accurate to say there are a bunch of fish in a school?* (yes) *Why?* (A school is a large group of fish.) *Is it also accurate to say there are a bunch of kids in most schools? Why?* (Yes, most schools teach large numbers of children at one time.)

Now revisit pages 20–21

Book Talk

- **Comprehension Strategy** Ask *What generalization does the author make about where fish live?* (Most fish live near the surface.) *How can you tell this is a generalization?* (It is a broad, general statement; it has the signal word *most* in it.)

- Ask *Does the deep sea anglerfish live near the surface?* (No, it lives in the deep sea.) *Do you think the deep sea anglerfish is a* predator? (yes) *Why?* (It eats smaller fish.)

Turn to page 22 – Book Talk

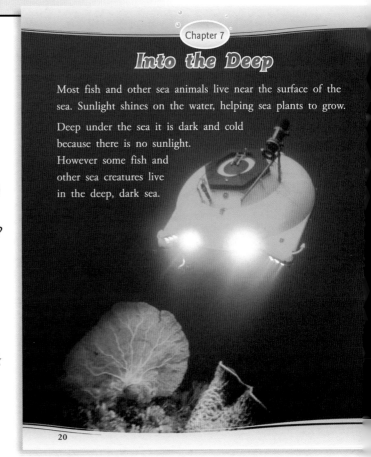

Chapter 7

Into the Deep

Most fish and other sea animals live near the surface of the sea. Sunlight shines on the water, helping sea plants to grow.

Deep under the sea it is dark and cold because there is no sunlight. However some fish and other sea creatures live in the deep, dark sea.

20

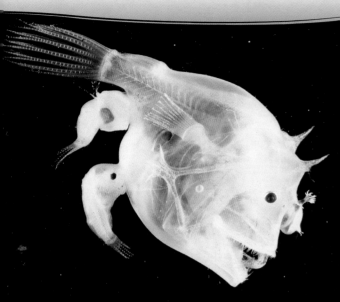

Deep Sea Anglerfish

Deep sea anglerfish live deep in the sea. Female deep sea anglerfish have glowing **lures** on their heads. Small sea animals swim to the glowing lures. Then the anglerfish eat the sea animals.

21

Future Vocabulary

- Ask *What fish lives in the deep sea?* (a deep sea anglerfish) *Does the deep sea anglerfish live with a* bunch *of other fish in the deep sea?* (no)

Now revisit pages 22–23

During Reading

Book Talk

- Leave this page spread for children to discover on their own when they read the book individually.

Turn to page 24 – Book Talk

Chapter 8

Coral Reefs

Coral reefs are some of the most beautiful places in the world. They are found in warm shallow seas. Coral reefs are made by millions of tiny sea creatures over thousands of years.

Lots of beautiful fish live around coral reefs. Many are brightly colored.

22

Clownfish

Clownfish live in warm places on coral reefs. They make their homes among the stinging **tentacles** of **sea anemones**. However the tentacles do not hurt them.

The stinging tentacles keep the clownfish fish safe from other bigger fish.

23

T0069

Future

- Ask ... the ... cles of the anemone ... sleek? (Yes, they look smooth and shiny.) *Would you want to touch them?* (No, they would sting.) *Do they sting the clownfish?* (No, the clownfish are safe in them.) *Does it look like the clownfish are zigzagging through the tentacles?* (yes) *How can you tell?* (They look like they are turning sharply.)

Go to page T5 —
Revisiting the Text

During Reading

Book Talk

- Note: Point out this text feature page as a reference for children's use while reading independently.

Individual Reading

Have each child read the entire book at his or her own pace while remaining in the group.

Go to page T5 — Revisiting the Text

Glossary

breed	to come together and make babies
cartilage	a type of hard body tissue that makes up the skeletons of some fish
coral reefs	hard hills near the top of the sea made out of the skeletons of tiny sea animals
freshwater	water that is not salty
gills	the parts of a fish, inside its body, that it breathes through
kelp	large, brown seaweed
life cycle	the different stages of a plant or animal's life
lures	objects used as bait to attract animals
marine	of the sea
native	local to a place or country
predator	an animal that hunts and eats other animals
sea anemones	sea creatures with tube-shaped bodies that are topped with stinging tentacles
shallow	not deep
tentacles	long growths on the head of an animal

Index

During independent work time, children can read the online book at: **www.rigbyflyingcolors.com**

Future Vocabulary

- Use the notes on the right-hand pages to develop oral vocabulary that goes beyond the text. These vocabulary words first appear in future texts. These words are: *sleek*, *bunch*, and *zigzag*.

Turn back to page 1

Reading Vocabulary Review
Activity Sheet: Vocabulary Anchor

- Have children write *skeleton* on the boat of the Vocabulary Anchor. Then have them choose a related word and write it on the anchor.

- Think aloud about how the two words are related. Have children write similarities and differences next to the plus and minus signs. Encourage children to make a connection with the new word and write their ideas on the sail.

Comprehension Strategy Review
Use Interactive Modeling Card: Main Idea and Supporting Details

- Discuss with children the book's central idea. Ask them to suggest details from different chapters that support the main idea.

- Record the main idea on the tabletop and supporting details on the legs.

Phonics Review

- Review the list of compound words introduced earlier. Have children volunteer any new compound words they remember from the book.

- Have children take turns reading the words listed.

Fluency Review

- Read aloud page 18, modeling pausing at the commas. Talk about how commas signal readers to pause. Have children read the page aloud to practice pausing.

- Partner children and have them take turns reading page 18. Remind them not to rush through sentences, but to take their time.

Reading-Writing Connection
Activity Sheet: Making Conclusions

To assist children with linking reading and writing:

- Model drawing a conclusion by reading a passage aloud, thinking aloud about the details, and then forming a conclusion. Have children use details from passages to make conclusions.

- Have children draw a picture that illustrates one of their conclusions.

Assessing Future Vocabulary

Work with each child individually. Ask questions that elicit each child's understanding of the Future Vocabulary words. Note each child's responses:

- Which item would you describe as sleek, a new car or an old blanket? Why?

- What are some things you would do if a bunch of your friends came over on a Saturday?

- What could you draw using a zigzag line?

Assessing Comprehension Strategy

Work with each child individually. Note each child's understanding of making generalizations:

- What examples can you use to support the generalization that all fish have skeletons?

- What generalization can you make about where fish live based on the examples the author gave?

- What is the value of making generalizations?

Assessing Phonics

Work with each child individually. Make word cards for the words *sometimes, sunlight, anglerfish, bluefin, predator, salmon,* and *fantastic.* Have each child find and read aloud the compound words. Then ask each child to identify the words that make up each compound. Have each child choose one of the compound words and use it in a sentence. Note each child's responses for understanding identifying and reading compound words:

- Did each child accurately identify and read all the compound words?

- Did each child identify the two smaller words within each compound?

- Was each child able to use a compound word in a sentence?

Assessing Fluency

Have each child point to the commas on page 16 and then read the page aloud. Note each child's understanding of pausing at commas:

- Did each child accurately identify all the commas on the page?

- Did each child pause at the commas?

- Did each child pause each time a comma appeared in sentences with multiple commas?

Interactive Modeling Cards

Classifying New Words

New Word	Noun (person, place, or thing)	Verb (action word)	Adjective or Adverb (describing word)
bunch	X	X	
sleek			X
zigzag	X	X	X

Directions: With children, fill in the Classifying New Words chart using the words *bunch*, *sleek*, and *zigzag*.

Main Idea and Supporting Details

Main Idea
Fish live all over the world.

Supporting Detail
They live in cold and warm places.

Supporting Detail
They live in rivers, lakes, and ponds.

Supporting Detail
They live close to shore and deep in the sea.

Supporting Detail
They live in salty seas.

Directions: With children, fill in the Main Idea and Supporting Details chart for *A World of Fish*.

Discussion Questions

- What do predator fish eat? (Literal)
- Why can small fish see the lure of the anglerfish in the deep sea? (Critical Thinking)
- Why do small fish that live near the shore hide in sea plants? (Inferential)

Activity Sheets

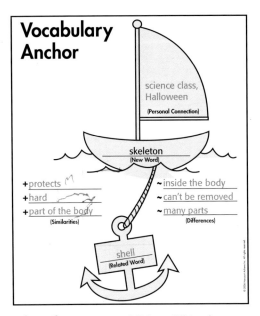

Vocabulary Anchor

science class, Halloween
(Personal Connection)

skeleton
(New Word)

+protects
+hard
+part of the body
(Similarities)

~inside the body
~can't be removed
~many parts
(Differences)

shell
(Related Word)

Directions: Have children fill in the Vocabulary Anchor using the word *skeleton*.

Making Conclusions

Conclusion	Details from the Book
Most freshwater fish cannot live in salty seas.	Freshwater fish need clean, fresh water to survive.
Most sharks are predators.	Most sharks hunt fish and other sea animals.
Kelp is helpful to fish.	Fish and other sea animals hide in kelp.

Directions: Have children fill in the Making Conclusions chart for *A World of Fish.*

Optional: On a separate sheet of paper, have children illustrate one of their conclusions from the chart.